GREAT MOMENTS IN SCIENCE

LOUIS PASTEUR ADVANCES MICROBIOLOGY

by Douglas Hustad

Content Consultant
Benjamin J. Burwitz, PhD
Staff Scientist 3
Vaccine and Gene Therapy Institute
Oregon Health and Science University

Core Library

An Imprint of Abdo Publishing
abdopublishing.com

abdopublishing.com

Published by Abdo Publishing, a division of ABDO, PO Box 398166, Minneapolis, Minnesota 55439. Copyright © 2016 by Abdo Consulting Group, Inc. International copyrights reserved in all countries. No part of this book may be reproduced in any form without written permission from the publisher. Core Library™ is a trademark and logo of Abdo Publishing.

Printed in the United States of America, North Mankato, Minnesota
092015
012016

Cover Photo: SuperStock/Glow Images
Interior Photos: SuperStock/Glow Images, 1; Nancy Nehring/iStockphoto, 4; Bettmann/Corbis, 7, 29, 39; Red Line Editorial, 11, 37; Rischgitz/Getty Images, 12; The Print Collector/Getty Images, 14; DEA/G. Dagli Orti/De Agostini/Getty Images, 19; Hulton Archives/Getty Images, 20; Photo12/UIG/Getty Images, 22; Alexandre Cabanel, 25; Science Source, 27; Centers for Disease Control and Prevention, 32, 45; Prisma/UIG/Getty Images, 35

Editor: Arnold Ringstad
Series Designer: Maggie Villaume

Library of Congress Control Number: 2015945761

Cataloging-in-Publication Data
Hustad, Douglas.
 Louis Pasteur advances microbiology / Douglas Hustad.
   p. cm. -- (Great moments in science)
 ISBN 978-1-68078-017-8 (lib. bdg.)
 Includes bibliographical references and index.
 1. Scientists--France--Juvenile literature. 2. Microbiologists--France--Juvenile literature.   I. Title.
 509.2--dc23
                                                                              2015945761

CONTENTS

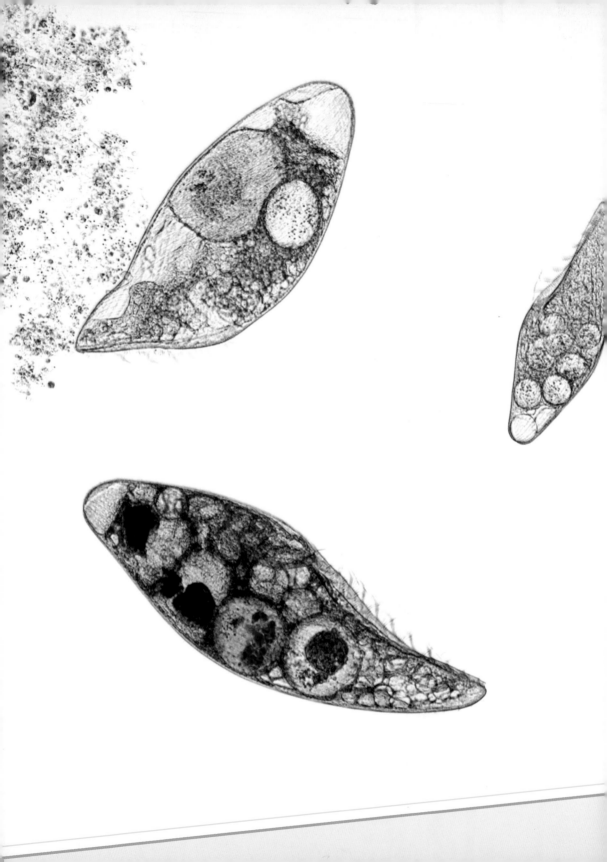

CHAPTER ONE

NOTHING SPONTANEOUS ABOUT IT

Louis Pasteur had been studying tiny creatures called microorganisms for years. He was not alone. By 1859 they were a subject of heavy debate. Scientists were trying to determine where they came from. A leading theory was spontaneous generation. This is the idea that life can come from nonliving matter. Early experiments seemed to show the idea was true. In the 1600s,

Scientists intensely studied microorganisms in the 1800s, but many questions about these tiny creatures remained.

scientist Jan Baptist van Helmont set out a jar filled with dirty cloth and corn. Mice soon appeared in the jar. He believed they had come from the materials in the jar. He did not realize they already existed. They simply were attracted to the jar.

People began questioning spontaneous generation before Pasteur's time. In 1668 an Italian named Francesco Redi attacked the idea. He performed an experiment to disprove it. Redi placed meat in three jars. The first was open. The second was partially sealed. The third was fully sealed. If spontaneous generation were real, flies and maggots should have been found in all three. But only the open jar had flies.

Challenges

Redi's experiment was a step forward. However, some thought it was too specific. They believed his results might apply only to meat. English scientist John Needham tried a similar experiment in 1745. He used a broth mixture. Needham boiled the liquid

In addition to studying spontaneous generation, Redi was a doctor and a poet.

G. Benaglia inc.

and sealed the containers. The liquids became cloudy, showing microorganisms growing inside. Needham believed this was proof of spontaneous generation.

But in 1768, another Italian scientist tested the theory. Lazzaro Spallanzani believed Needham's liquid was contaminated before the container was sealed.

So he boiled his liquid in an already-sealed container. Nothing grew inside it.

This still was not enough proof for some people. Critics believed Spallanzani showed the theory to be only partially untrue. Believers in spontaneous generation thought the process needed air to occur.

Developing Research

Around the year 1700, the microscope was invented. The device allowed people to see microorganisms. Many believed they were the product of spontaneous generation. They thought the theory might not apply to large animals. But perhaps these tiny creatures could arise from nothing.

By the late 1850s, this belief was still widely held. The Academy of Sciences in France announced a contest to see who could support or refute it. The prize was 2,500 Francs. This was a small fortune at the time. Pasteur had a great opportunity to prove his theory. If he won, the prize money could also fund more research.

He believed he knew where other scientists had gone wrong. Pasteur set out to show that no life arose out of a liquid even when it was exposed to air. This would be strong evidence against spontaneous generation.

The Swan-Necked Flask

Pasteur compared two types of bottles. One was a regular flask with a top exposed to the air. The other had the same kind of bottom. But Pasteur bent its opening into a long, S-shaped neck.

The bottle would allow air to touch the liquid. But dust or other particles would not be able to drift into it.

Pasteur boiled the liquid to kill existing microorganisms. He then allowed it to sit. For weeks, months, and even years, he observed several of these flasks. He tried them in different locations. He even tested some in the mountains.

The bottles with S-shaped necks remained clear of microbial life. But if the neck were broken, microorganisms would start to grow. The same thing happened if the bottle was tipped over.

Still Crystal Clear

It was important for Pasteur to test his flasks for as long as possible. He wanted to show time was not a factor. Spontaneous generation would not happen no matter how long the flasks sat. In a way, these experiments are still proving true. A flask believed to have been used by Pasteur in 1864 now resides at the Science Museum of London. The liquid inside remains clear to this day.

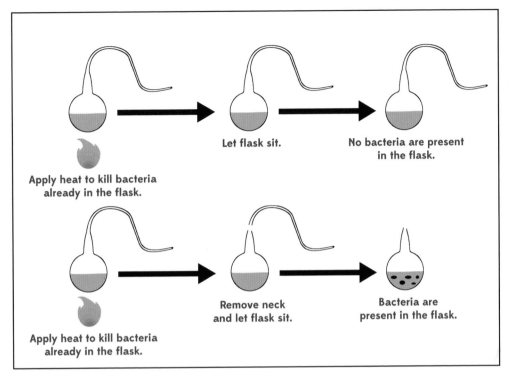

Apply heat to kill bacteria already in the flask.

Let flask sit.

No bacteria are present in the flask.

Apply heat to kill bacteria already in the flask.

Remove neck and let flask sit.

Bacteria are present in the flask.

The Flask Experiment

This graphic shows a basic overview of how Pasteur conducted his experiments into spontaneous generation. It also shows the results. What is the main difference between the two experiments? How does this graphic further your understanding about what Pasteur figured out?

Winning the Contest

Pasteur was able to easily win the prize in 1862. His experiments were more thorough than those of other challengers. Pasteur's experimental design allowed him to get consistent results. But some people held

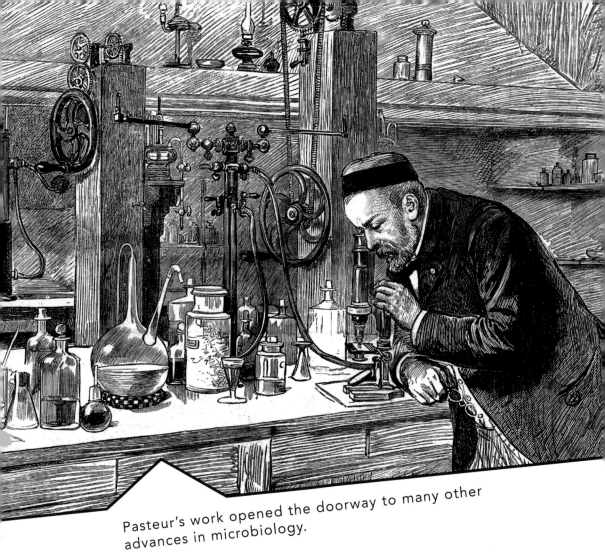

Pasteur's work opened the doorway to many other advances in microbiology.

on to their belief in spontaneous generation. They were not convinced by Pasteur's work.

One of the biggest challenges was with air quality. Some of Pasteur's critics claimed they had found air samples with no germs in them. So how would this air spoil a liquid? This caused Pasteur to reconsider. He had believed germs were everywhere. He changed his view to the idea that some places have more germs than others.

Pasteur presented his claims at a lecture in 1864. He stated once and for all that life was not generated spontaneously. Instead, it came from other life. He believed anyone who thought otherwise was influenced by poor experiments. But Pasteur recognized his findings were about more than disputing bad experiments. It was the start of his germ theory of disease. This theory would soon greatly advance the field of microbiology.

EXPLORE ONLINE

The website below presents beliefs about spontaneous generation from before Pasteur's experiments. What new information or evidence was presented?

Spontaneous Generation

mycorelibrary.com/microbiology

EARLY STUDIES IN CHEMISTRY

Pasteur was born on December 27, 1822, in Dole, France. His father was a war veteran who made leather out of animal hides. Pasteur's parents wanted their son to have a successful life. They had little money, but they made sure he received a good education.

The young Pasteur showed interest in the creative arts. He loved painting. He often made portraits

Pasteur's early work was in chemistry, but it later expanded to biology, medicine, and other fields.

of friends and neighbors. People in town thought he could have made a career as an artist. But as he got older, he put the paintbrush aside and concentrated on his studies.

Pasteur was a chemistry student. While at college in 1845, he worked closely with Professor Antoine Jérôme Balard. Balard believed Pasteur had a lot of potential. Under Balard's influence, Pasteur dedicated himself to chemistry.

Pasteur worked as Balard's assistant for two years. In 1848 he became a professor of physics at a university in Dijon, France. He researched crystals and their effects on light. In 1854, at age 32, he was named Dean of the Faculty of Science at Lille University in northern France.

Experiments with Fermentation

Northern France was known for its wine industry. This inspired Pasteur to begin researching fermentation. The fermentation process was essential to making alcoholic beverages, such as wine. It was not fully understood at this time.

In 1856 a businessman in Lille came asking for Pasteur's help. His name was M. Bigo, and he had problems with his beet juice spoiling. Instead of becoming alcohol, it was turning sour. Pasteur went to visit Bigo's factory to help him.

Pasteur observed the fermentation process. He found the juice in some tanks turned out fine, whereas the juice in other tanks turned sour. The sour tanks had a layer of slime on top. Pasteur was puzzled.

He wanted to find out what the difference was. This was the start of his experiments with fermentation.

In the good samples, he saw yeast. This is a key ingredient in fermentation. But in the bad samples, there was something else. There were differently shaped organisms. Pasteur guessed they must have made the yeast ineffective. These bacteria produced acid instead of alcohol.

Discovering Bacteria

Pasteur did not know how to kill the bacteria. But he knew how to prevent

Pasteur's work with fermentation laid the groundwork for his future studies.

Pasteur used specialized brewing equipment in his work on fermentation.

them from appearing. The tanks had to be kept clean. They also had to be cleaned between uses. Pasteur's advice worked.

Pasteur became famous locally. The wine industry was very important, and Pasteur had aided it greatly. He continued his work on fermentation, and he published a paper on it the next year.

This was the foundation of Pasteur's future work. His studies of microorganisms and fermentation led to his later ideas on spontaneous generation. The work formed the basis of his germ theory of disease that followed much later.

FURTHER EVIDENCE

Chapter Two discusses Pasteur's early research into fermentation. What was one of the main points of this chapter? What evidence is included to support this point? Read the article at the website below. Find a quote from the article that supports a main point of the chapter.

Pasteur and Fermentation
mycorelibrary.com/microbiology

CHAPTER THREE

PASTEURIZATION

In 1857 Pasteur moved to Paris, France. He continued his experiments with fermentation. He also began researching spontaneous generation. The two were related. Pasteur came to discover microorganisms explained both processes. It seemed possible they also explained many other things.

No one understood why foods and drinks spoiled. People at the time considered them diseased. Pasteur

One of Pasteur's homes in Paris has been preserved as a museum.

started investigating diseased wine while on vacation in 1858. This research aided his discrediting of spontaneous generation.

Pasteur was a major authority on microorganisms. In 1863 the emperor of France, Napoleon III, asked for his help. He wanted Pasteur to continue studying spoiled wine to help France's wine industry. Pasteur set up a new lab for this research.

He had been experimenting with ways to kill bacteria in wine. He found heating it to 154 degrees Fahrenheit (68°C) for 30 minutes would prevent the wine from spoiling. This process became known as pasteurization. People soon realized it could be used for milk as well. It is still used today to keep drinks and foods safe.

Saving Silkworms

In 1865 another French industry was in trouble. This time it was a problem with silkworms. France was one of the largest producers of silk in the world. But a strange disease was affecting the silkworms.

Napoleon III was the nephew of Napoleon I, the French leader known for conquering much of Europe in the early 1800s.

Some were dying. Others simply were not producing enough silk.

Pasteur believed he could help. At first he planned to destroy the silkworms used in the manufacturing process. He hoped that would kill the disease. New silkworms would be fine. But he soon discovered even healthy worms could pass on the disease.

Pasteur's research went on for three years. He found there were two disease-causing microorganisms living inside each worm. These diseases could spread through silkworm populations without being noticed. Once Pasteur's team could see the microorganisms, they could eliminate the diseased worms. For solving this problem, Pasteur became a national hero. He also received a large cash prize.

Proving the Germ Theory

Pasteur's research had led him to establish that microorganisms, also called germs, were responsible for disease. This theory was challenged for a few

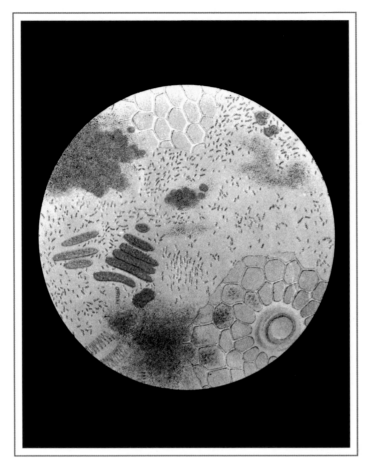

Looking through microscopes, Pasteur's team was able to figure out the mysteries of the silkworm diseases.

reasons. First, it was new. Many people thought they already understood what caused disease. Second, Pasteur was not a doctor. This made people reluctant to believe him.

But Joseph Lister was a doctor. He was a surgeon who read Pasteur's work in the early 1860s. At that time, hospitals did not take the anti-germ steps they take today. Doctors did not wash their hands. Instruments were not cleaned after use. Lister decided to put Pasteur's ideas into action.

He chose a type of acid that would kill germs. He used it to clean instruments and wounds. At first the acid was irritating to the skin. It did more harm than good. But after experimentation, he found a mixture that worked. Patients got fewer infections. Lister published a paper on his findings in 1867. In it, he thanked Pasteur

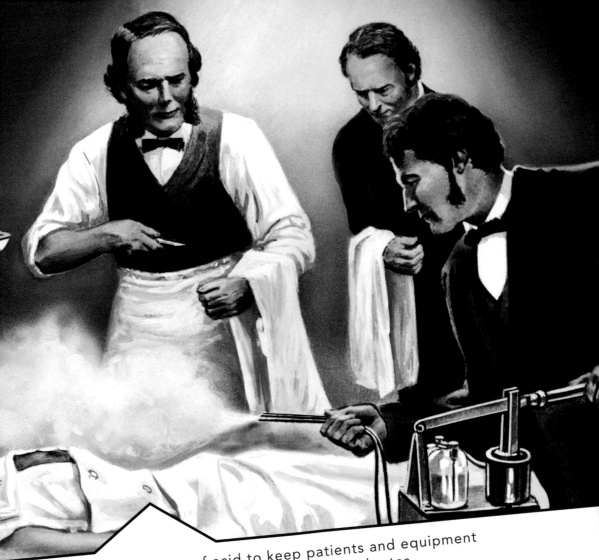

Lister's use of acid to keep patients and equipment clean dramatically improved survival rates.

for discovering germs as one of the basic causes of disease.

Other surgeons were still skeptical. But numbers proved Lister and Pasteur right. Before the new

Personal Experiences

In the 1860s, Pasteur experienced great personal loss. His father died in 1865. Then he lost two daughters to typhoid fever in 1866. In 1868, Pasteur had a broken blood vessel in his brain. Part of the left side of his body was paralyzed. But Pasteur kept working through all of this.

The Franco-German War (1870–1871) gave him an opportunity to put his medical ideas into action. Pasteur saw wounded French soldiers dying of disease and infection. He vowed to do something about it. He forced the medical corps to adopt his ideas about the sterilization of instruments. In 1873 Pasteur was admitted to the French Academy of Medicine.

methods, 46 percent of patients who had limbs amputated died. Afterward, that statistic dropped to 15 percent. Lister's contribution to medical history lives on with the product Listerine. He did not invent the popular germ-killing mouthwash, but it was named in his honor.

The following passage is from an 1895 *New York Times* article looking back at the development of the germ theory of disease:

> A very important chapter in the history of bacteriological progress would be omitted if no reference should be made to the notable discoveries and achievements of Pasteur in the field of fermentation. The importance of his researches in this field will be seen when it's recalled that they preceded Davaine's discovery by some years, as he began to publish his conclusions in 1857. Pasteur's study of the ferments related directly to the defense of certain agricultural and commercial products against injurious invasion by parasitic organisms, but, indirectly, they were of great service in developing that branch of bacteriology which deals with the pathogenic or disease-producing bacteria. . . . The researches of Pasteur cleared up their history, pointed out their functions, and were of great commercial value.

> Source: "Hunting the Bacteria." New York Times. New York Times, February 3, 1895. Web. 13 July 2015.

What's the Big Idea?

Take a close look at this passage. What is the main connection being made between fermentation and the germ theory of disease? What was it about fermentation that led Pasteur to a greater understanding of disease?

CHAPTER FOUR

VACCINATION AND CURING DISEASES

Pasteur was not done saving French industries. In 1876 a serious disease called anthrax was killing sheep and cattle. Robert Koch had identified the bacteria that caused the illness.

Pasteur began to experiment with a treatment. He found he could weaken the disease by heating it. If he kept the bacteria at approximately 108 degrees

Anthrax is caused by a bacterium named *Bacillus anthracis.*

Fahrenheit (42°C) for two weeks, it would not be as powerful. He believed when exposed to this weakened disease, the body's immune system would be able to defeat it. He called this weakened form of the disease a *vaccine*. The word came from the Latin *vacca*, meaning "cow." English doctor Edward Jenner had done research on a vaccine for the disease smallpox, which is related to the disease cowpox, many years earlier.

In 1881 Pasteur and his team injected the vaccine into 31 animals. Another set of 31 animals was given no injection. Then, after a few weeks, the team injected the full strength anthrax into all the animals. All but one of the animals that had received the vaccine survived. Most of the others died. Pasteur's vaccine was distributed around the country. Anthrax was almost completely eliminated.

A Happy Accident

Pasteur also tested vaccines on chickens. An outbreak of chicken cholera was killing many birds. Pasteur

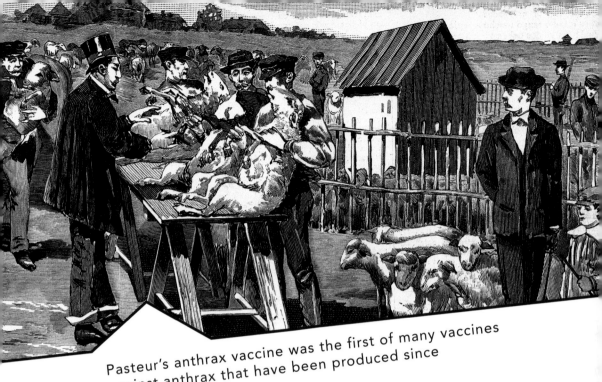

Pasteur's anthrax vaccine was the first of many vaccines against anthrax that have been produced since the 1880s.

tried to find a vaccine that would work. He was discouraged, as his results were not very effective. But he continued working. He knew chance favored the prepared mind.

Pasteur instructed one of his assistants, Charles Chamberland, to inject some chickens with the cholera virus. But Chamberland forgot and went on vacation. He did not return until a month later. The virus had sat there untouched the whole time. Chamberland decided to inject the chickens with it

Charles Edouard Chamberland

Pasteur revolutionized microbiology, but he did not do it alone. Chamberland first met Pasteur as a student at the École Normale in 1875. The two men worked together until Pasteur's death in 1895. Chamberland had a hand in many of Pasteur's most famous discoveries. During the anthrax research, Chamberland produced the vaccines as he traveled the country giving the doses to sheep. When Pasteur founded the Pasteur Institute, Chamberland was put in charge of bacteriology research. Chamberland died in 1908.

anyway. They got sick but soon recovered. He thought it must have been a mistake. He was going to throw the virus sample away. But Pasteur stopped him.

Pasteur realized that by sitting untouched, the virus must have gotten weaker. It could then be used as a vaccine. Pasteur again was considered a hero. He received the highest honor in France, the Grand Cross of the Legion of Honor.

Rabies Research

By the 1880s, Pasteur had shown vaccines were

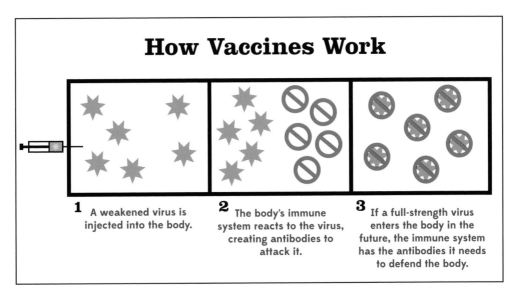

How Vaccines Work

1 A weakened virus is injected into the body.

2 The body's immune system reacts to the virus, creating antibodies to attack it.

3 If a full-strength virus enters the body in the future, the immune system has the antibodies it needs to defend the body.

How Vaccines Work

This diagram gives a basic overview of how vaccines work. Does this help you better understand the discussion of vaccines in Chapter Four?

effective at stopping disease in animals. But he had not yet shown any results in humans. This would soon change with Pasteur's research into rabies. Rabies at the time was known as hydrophobia, meaning fear of water. This is because of the symptoms people showed. Rabies victims were known to avoid drinking water due to throat pain.

Rabies was not a common disease in humans. A person could get it only from an infected animal. In humans it usually was deadly. At that time, people thought only dogs carried rabies. But Pasteur found it in rabbits and monkeys. It was more widespread than commonly believed.

Pasteur drew the virus directly from a sick animal, usually a dog. He then dried a sample of it for several days. This weakened the virus for use in a vaccine. By 1885 it was ready for its first human test.

A Big Risk

On July 6, 1885, the first test case for the rabies vaccine showed up on Pasteur's doorstop. Nine-year-old Joseph Meister had been attacked by a rabies-carrying dog. He had bites all over his body. His parents knew Pasteur had been working on a treatment for rabies. They rushed the boy to see the famous scientist.

Pasteur was hesitant about the procedure. This would be the first test on a person. And Pasteur was not a doctor. There was considerable risk. But a doctor on Pasteur's team told him the boy was sure

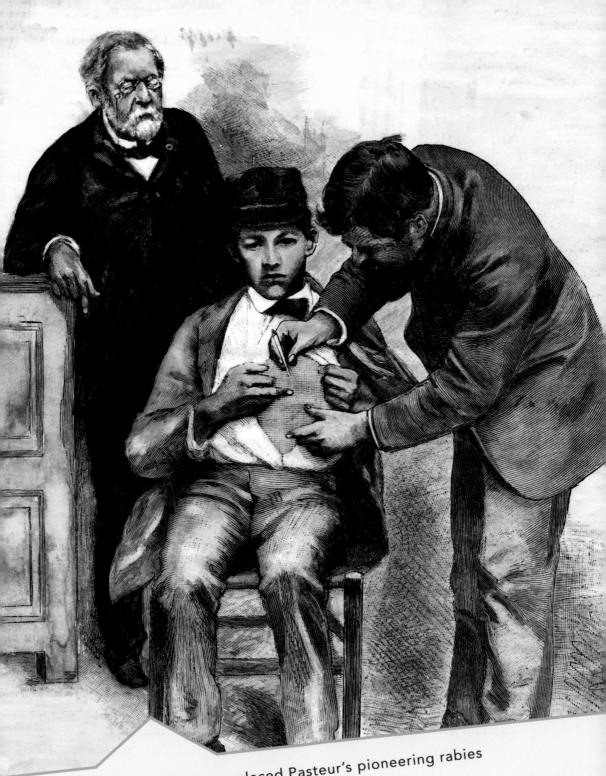

Later scientists replaced Pasteur's pioneering rabies vaccine with safer versions.

The Pasteur Institute

In 1888 Pasteur opened the Pasteur Institute to expand his research. The first location was in Paris, but others opened around the world. The institute studied diseases, including rabies, as well as other issues in microbiology. Pasteur's health was declining by the time the institute opened. He died in 1895. Today the institute continues his mission of research. There are now 32 more locations worldwide.

to die without treatment. So Pasteur injected the first dose.

Joseph got 12 more shots in the next several days. He never developed rabies, and he soon was able to go back home. With this success, Pasteur began making large amounts of the vaccine. Patients began flocking to his laboratory to be treated. His understanding of microbiology and viruses changed the way we think about disease. His contributions remain important parts of our modern world. Millions of lives have been saved thanks to Pasteur's experiments and discoveries.

Swedish doctor Axel Munthe was present during some of Pasteur's work with rabies. He wrote about how Pasteur obtained samples of the disease:

> In these kennels were kept forty rabid dogs. The handling of these dogs, all foaming with rage, was a very dangerous affair, and I often marveled at the courage displayed by everybody. Pasteur himself was absolutely fearless. Anxious to secure a sample of saliva straight from the jaws of a rabid dog, I once saw him with a glass tube held between his lips draw a few drops of the deadly saliva from the mouth of a rabid bull-dog, held on the table by two assistants, their hands protected by leather gloves.

Source: Alex Munthe. "The Story of San Michele." Internet Archive. Internet Archive, n.d. Web. July 13, 2015

Point of View

The writer views Pasteur as very courageous and willing to take risks to further his research. Read back through this chapter. Do you agree Pasteur was a risk taker? What evidence can you find for or against this idea?

IMPORTANT DATES

1822

Louis Pasteur is born in Dole, France.

1845

Pasteur studies under Antoine Balard at the École Normale.

1856

Pasteur meets M. Bigo and begins research on fermentation.

1873

Pasteur is admitted into the French Academy of Medicine for his work on disease and infection.

1876

Pasteur begins research on an anthrax vaccine.

1881

Pasteur's anthrax vaccine is tested and shown effective.

1862

Pasteur wins a prize for his work on spontaneous generation.

1865

Pasteur discovers the cause of, and cure for, a disease killing France's silkworms.

1867

Joseph Lister publishes a paper based on Pasteur's research, showing sterilization of instruments prevents infection in hospitals.

1885

Pasteur administers a vaccine to a human for the first time, treating nine-year-old Joseph Meister for rabies.

1888

The Pasteur Institute opens.

1895

Pasteur dies in Paris at the age of 72.

STOP AND THINK

Surprise Me

Chapter One discusses some early theories about germs before Pasteur's research. What two or three were the most surprising? Write a few sentences about each fact. Why did you find each fact surprising?

Dig Deeper

After reading this book, what questions do you still have about Pasteur and microbiology? With an adult's help, find a few reliable sources that can help you answer your questions. Write a paragraph about what you learned.

Take a Stand

In Pasteur's time, medical testing on animals was common. Now there are lots of rules about what kind of testing can and cannot be done on animals. Do you think it is okay to test on animals? Why or why not? What sort of rules should be in place if testing is okay?

You Are There

This book discusses Pasteur's groundbreaking research into microbiology, which was very new at the time. Imagine you're hearing Pasteur give a lecture in the mid-1800s. Would you believe him right away? Or would you hold on to your old beliefs? Write a diary entry with your thoughts.

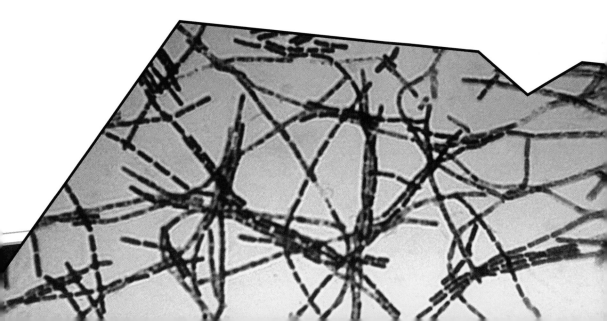

GLOSSARY

amputated
removed surgically

bacteria
a type of microorganism that
can cause disease

chemistry
the study of substances and
what they are made of

contaminated
to make impure by adding a
substance

fermentation
the chemical process that
turns liquid into alcohol

flask
a type of glass bottle used
for lab experiments

laboratory
a space for scientific
experiments

microbiology
the study of microscopic
organisms

microorganism
any organism that is too small
to be seen with the naked
eye

organism
a life form

physics
the study of energy, motion,
and force

sterilization
a process that destroys germs
that live on surfaces

virus
an infectious disease

yeast
a living organism that is a key
component of fermentation

LEARN MORE

Books

Basher, Simon. *Basher Science: Microbiology*. New York: Kingfisher, 2015.

Brown, Jordan. *Micro Mania*. New York: Imagine, 2009.

Websites

To learn more about Great Moments in Science, visit **booklinks.abdopublishing.com**. These links are routinely monitored and updated to provide the most current information available.

Visit **mycorelibrary.com** for free additional tools for teachers and students.

INDEX

ABOUT THE AUTHOR

Douglas Hustad is a children's author from Minneapolis, Minnesota. He has written several books on science for young people.